Eleanor Wint

Ilustrations by

Lukasz Poduch

Order this book online at www.trafford.com
or email orders@trafford.com

Most Trafford titles are also available at major online book retailers.

© Copyright 2012 Eleanor Wint.

All rights reserved. No part of this publication may be reproduced, stored in a retrieval system, or transmitted, in any form or by any means, electronic, mechanical, photocopying, recording, or otherwise, without the written prior permission of the author.

Printed in the United States of America.

ISBN: 978-1-4669-5620-9 (sc)
978-1-4669-5619-3 (e)

Library of Congress Control Number: 2012916263

Trafford rev. 10/12/2012

 www.trafford.com

North America & international
toll-free: 1 888 232 4444 (USA & Canada)
phone: 250 383 6864 ♦ fax: 812 355 4082

FOREWORD

Marcus Garvey's life mission was the upliftment of Africans at home and abroad. Marcus and his wife, Amy, wanted to change the way we thought about ourselves. To this end, they published a book of Garvey's teachings, The Philosophy and Opinions of Marcus Garvey, some of which have been collected in Marcus Teaches Us.

By providing children with the ideas of Marcus Garvey such as "Africans all over the world must unite to be strong," our children now have the opportunity to ponder the wisdom of a hero who looks like us. In the pages of Marcus Teaches Us, our children will learn about Garvey's birthplace through a writing exercise, and there is an illustration of him standing in front of his childhood home in St. Ann's Bay, Jamaica.

Another remarkable feature of this book is the linking of Marcus Garvey to other heroes in the struggle for human dignity. For example, the children are encouraged to match the names of Harriet Tubman, Rosa Parks, and Louise Bennett with their pictures. The inclusion of these role models in a book written by a female scholar of Marcus Garvey sends the understated message that neither gender nor ethnicity is a barrier to greatness.

Marcus Teaches Us is also filled with images of children of African descent as well as activities to broaden their knowledge about the geography of Jamaica and Africa. Marcus Teaches us also sends a subtle message in the naming exercise of the continents where one of the ships of Marcus Garvey's Black Star Line sits proudly atop the globe. In addition, children are invited to complete pictures of animals such as giraffes, antelopes, and, of course, lions!

Marcus Garvey's dedication to the improvement of the lives of Africans is a memory that endears him to many parents. Marcus Teaches Us continues that grand tradition of teachers who passed along wisdom from one generation to the next. Baba Garvey would have been proud.

Geoffrey Philp
Blog: http://geoffreyphilp.blogspot.com/
Follow me on Twitter: @geoffreyphilp
Visit my Amazon page: http://amzn.to/A7oZgU
Geoffrey Philp is a poet and fiction writer who teaches English at Miami Dade College, where he also chairs the College Preparatory Department. A critically acclaimed author of over 12 books, Geoffrey's work been published in the Oxford Book of Caribbean Short Stories and the Oxford Book of Caribbean Verse. He has also won many awards for his poetry and fiction, including a Florida Individual Artist Fellowship, Sauza "Stay Pure" Award, James Michener Fellowships from the University of Miami, and in 2008, he won the coveted "Outstanding Writer" prize from the Jamaica Cultural Development Commission.

Testimonials

"This is an interpretation of Marcus Garvey's teachings for children of the preschool age. It is a very worthwhile effort and something all children will enjoy. It is beautifully illustrated and contains lots of activities that kids will love. A must for 3-6 year olds."

Tony Martin, Emeritus Professor of Africana Studies, Wellesley College, author of Marcus Garvey, Hero and author/compiler of The New Marcus Garvey Library.

"From my childhood my Aunty Viola Anderson taught me about Marcus Garvey. She taught me to love my black self and passed on all Marcus Garvey taught her while growing up. Therefore I was inclined to read the philosophy and the story of Marcus Garvey and his works. It is a privilege to be in Ghana, where I have visited Marcus Garvey's office in Accra. I am very happy that you have written this book for all to read. It's not only for kids. Adults also need to read it.
"If you don't know your past, you won't know your future." Ziggy Marley".

**Rastafari.
One God, One Aim, One Destiny.
Ganette Mariam (Mrs. Rita Marley OD.)**

This is my book.
I am ....

This is me...

Paste your picture or draw yourself!

I live in ....
with my ....

Can you colour the picture?
Try to draw something in! Flowers on the ground? Litlle circles on the dress? Be creative!

Marcus Garvey
was born
on the 17th August, 1887
in St. Ann's Bay,
Jamaica.
He was a printer.

He teaches us –
One Love
One God
One Aim
One Destiny
for us all.

Marcus Mosiah Garvey is a hero of Blacks at home and abroad.

He said,
Africans
all over the world
must unite
to be
strong.

He said
that
Africans need
to have
their own

ships,

factories,

stores,

everything.

Marcus Garvey urged us

to love one another

His mission took his message all over the world.

Can you write in the names of the Continents?

Can you write the names on this page next to the correct faces on the page over there?

1. H.I.M. Haile Selassie I

2. Louise Bennett (Miss Lou)

3. Hariett Tubman

4. Martin Luther King, Jr

5. Ziggy Marley

6. Barrack Obama

7. Rosa Parks

YOUR ACTIVITY PAGE →

Marcus Garvey
is a
national Hero
of Jamaica
and a hero
of the World.

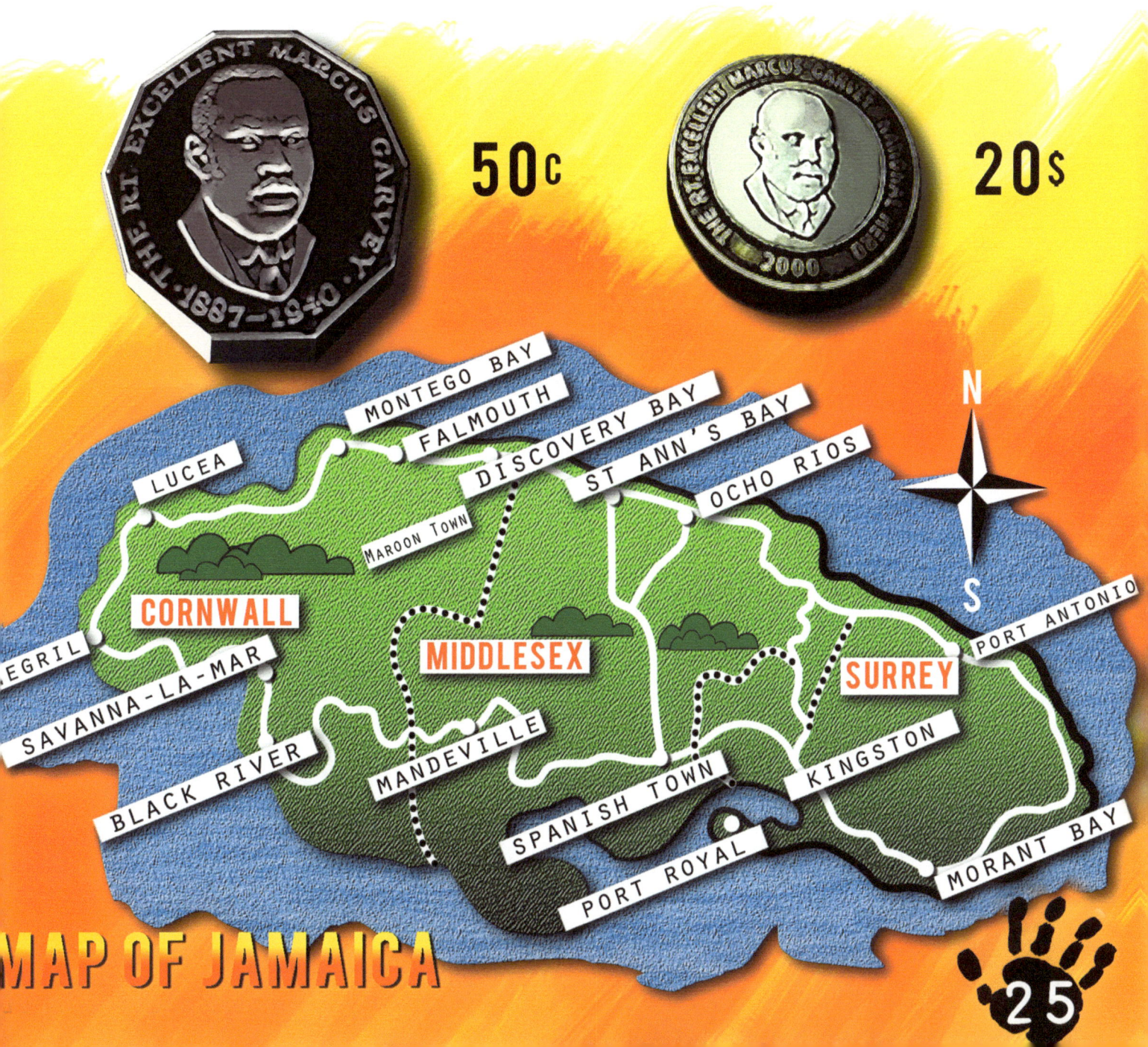

Marcus Garvey says...

Say! Africa for the Africans
Like America for the Americans
This the rallying cry for a nation
be it peace or revolution.

Europe cries to Europeans, ho!
Asiatics claim Asia, so
Australia for Australians
And Africa for the Africans.

Look at the picture made by your friends in Jamaica!
With a little work everyone can do beautifull things! Even you!

Dread-naught sailing over the main
Conscious of the Negus it came
Telling us of the sovereign true
Telling us of the Red, Black
　　　　and Green.
O Bravo! Garvey
Brave and true
His nature is of a Negro true
Voices shall see
Voices shall hear
That African Son, Equality.

by Marcus Garvey

Can you help me colour the picture?

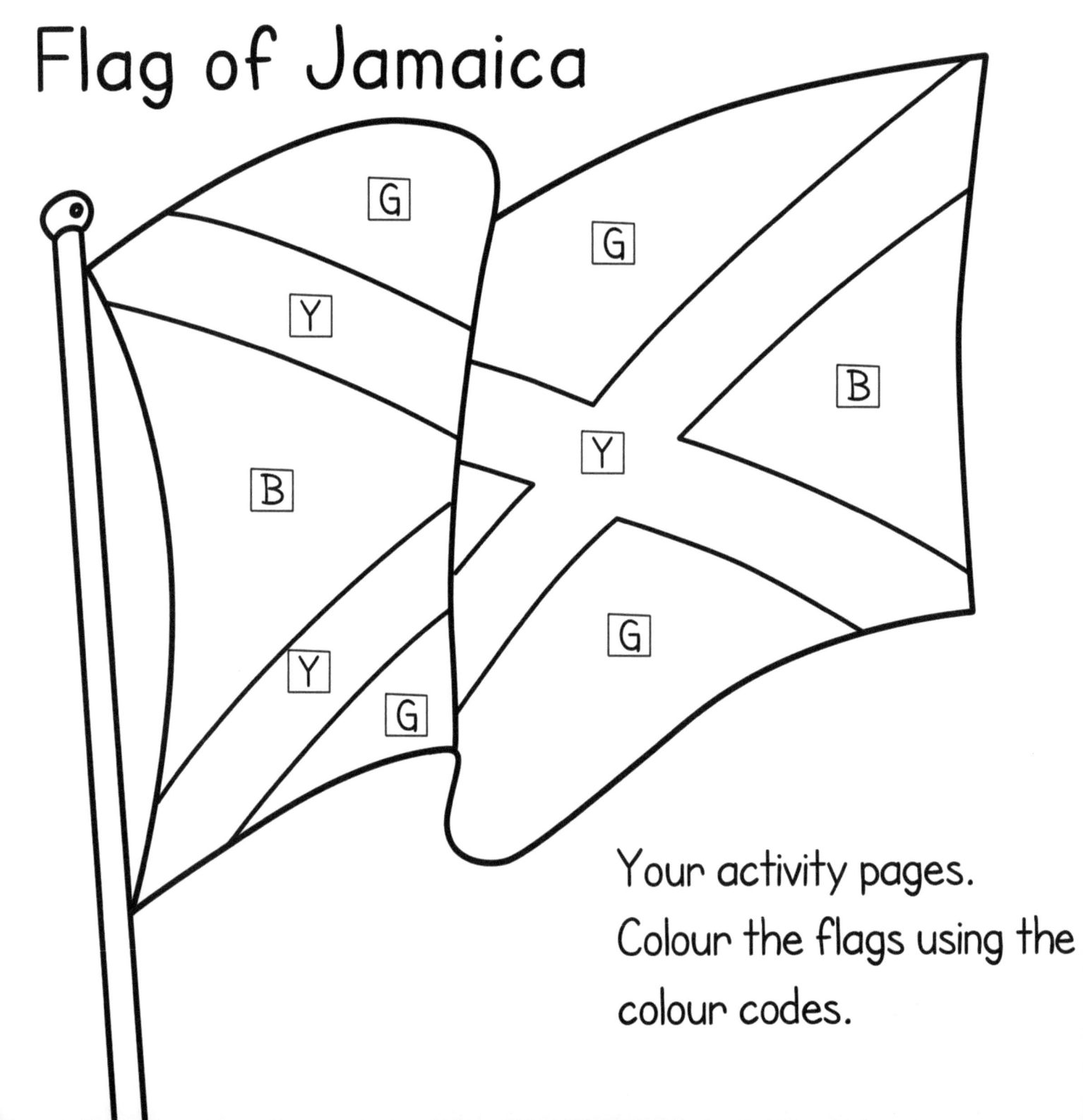

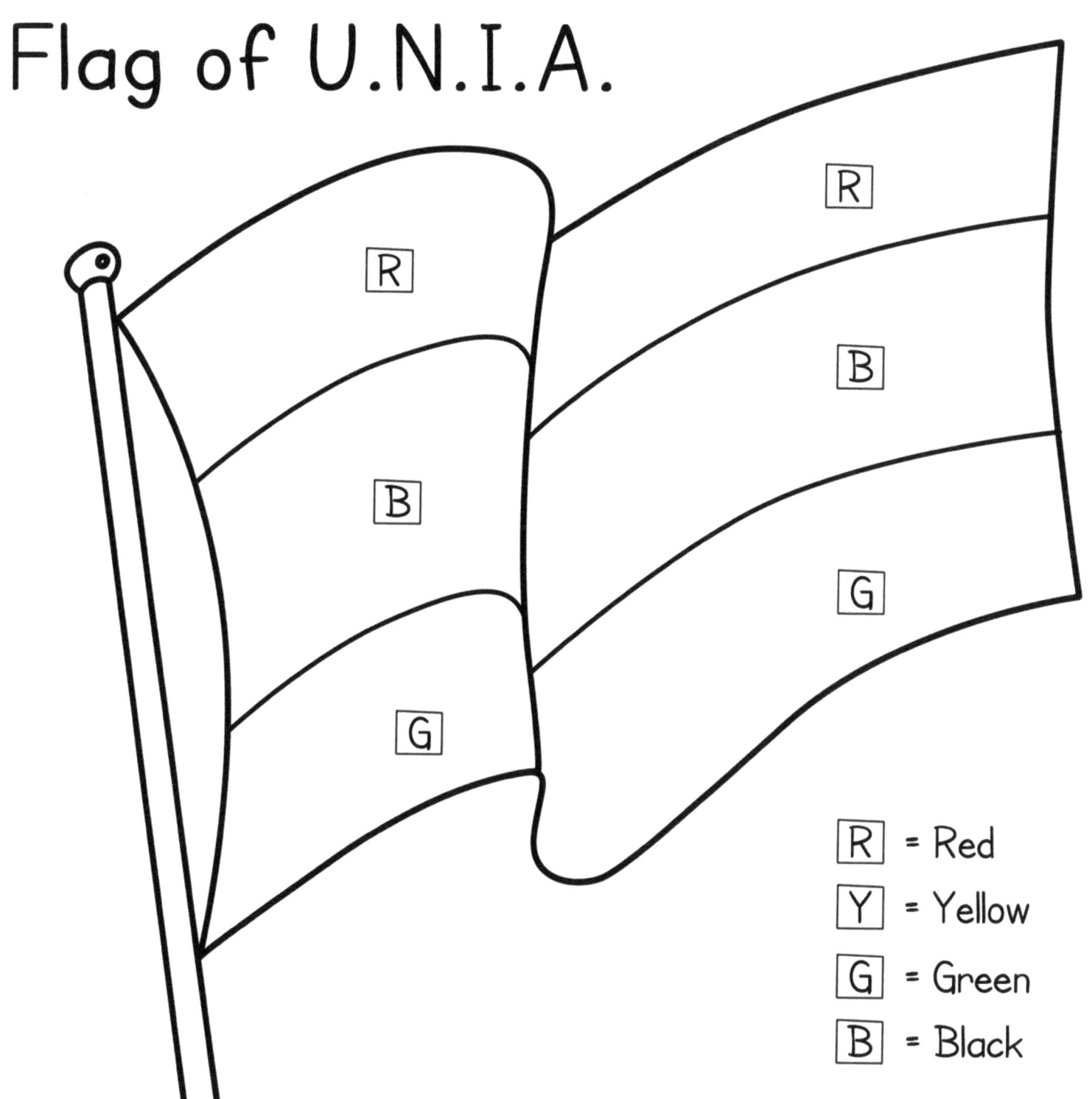

CPSIA information can be obtained
at www.ICGtesting.com
Printed in the USA
LVHW07n2259280818
588445LV00002B/3/P